COUNTRY FACT FILES

# France

## Véronique Bussolin

TURRIFF ACADEMY
LIBRARY

MACDONALD YOUNG BOOKS

First published in 1994 by Simon & Schuster Young Books
© Simon & Schuster Young Books 1994. Reprinted in 1996 and
1997 by Macdonald Young Books

First published in paperback in Great Britain in 1997 and reprinted in 1999 by
Macdonald Young Books

Macdonald Young Books, an imprint of Wayland Publishers Ltd
61 Western Road
Hove
East Sussex
BN3 1JD

| | |
|---|---|
| **Design** | Roger Kohn |
| **Editor** | Diana Russell |
| **DTP editor** | Helen Swansbourne |
| **Picture research** | Valerie Mulcahy |
| **Illustration** | Malcolm Porter |
| | János Márffy |
| **Consultant** | David Barrs |
| **Comissioning Editor** | Debbie Fox |

We are grateful to the following for permission
to reproduce photographs:
Front cover: Marco Polo (P H Halle) *below*, Marco Polo
(F Bouillot) *above*; Airbus Industrie, page 34 *above*; The.
Casement Collection/TRIP, pages 17, 28; Colorsport, page 21
*below*; Explorer, pages 11 *above* (François Jourdan), 18 (Luc
Girard), 25 *above* (Michel Garnier), 27 *right* (Alain Philippon),
42 *below* (Daniel Mar); Greenpeace, pages 38 (Gleizes),
40 (Dorreboon); Robert Harding Picture Library, pages 13
*above,* 27, *left (*Explorer), 30; Magnum, pages 11 *below* (Bruno
Barbey), 19 (Steve McCurry), 20 (Bruno Barbey), 29 *right*
(Jean Gaumy), 43 (ESA); Marco Polo, pages 8, 23, 29 *left,*
33 *below*, 35 (P H Halle), 15, 26, 34, *below* (F Bouillot);
Picturepoint, pages 8–9, 10, 22 above, 24, 36; Renault, page
37; Rex Features, pages 22 *below* (Aslan/Barth/Toussaint),
25 *below*, 31; Helene Rogers/TRIP, page 25 *centre*: Sefton
Photo library/TRIP, page 33 above; Tony Stone Worldwide,
page 41 (Thomas Zimmerman); Sygma, pages 14 (Yves
Virgile), 32 (John van Hasselt), 39 ( J M Turpin); The Walt
Disney Company, page 42 *above*; Zefa, page 12
(P Streichan), 13 *below*, 21 *above* (Rosenfield).

The statistics given in this book are the most up to date
available at the time of going to press.

Printed in Hong Kong by Wing King Tong Ltd

A CIP catalogue record for this book is available from the British Library

ISBN: 0 7500 2449 6

Words that are explained in the glossary are printed in
SMALL CAPITALS the first time they are mentioned in the text.

# ▄▄ INTRODUCTION

France has a very ancient history indeed. People living in caves settled in the southern part of the country nearly a million years ago. Much later, in about 500 AD, a group of people from the north of Europe conquered the land. These people, who were probably Scandinavians, were called the Franks and they gave their name to the country. For the next few hundred years, France was divided into several small kingdoms. But, over the centuries, these were joined together to form one country, ruled by one king.

During the Middle Ages, Paris became a centre of culture. Many Europeans envied its university, which was built in the 13th century. All over the country, churches, monasteries and huge cathedrals were built. From this time on, the economy, which was based on agriculture, expanded and France gradually opened itself to the rest of the world. It acquired colonies overseas and invested in commerce and industry at home.

The 20th century has brought many changes. France has fought two world wars and lost many colonies. It has invested a great deal in building its industrial power and its economy is now the fifth largest in the world – that is, the value of all the goods it produces is the world's fifth highest. During this period, people from Italy, Poland, Russia, Spain and North Africa have settled in the country and today they represent 7% of the total population. Sixty years ago half of the French population lived in the countryside; nowadays more than seven out of 10 people live in a town or city.

France is one of the most visited places

▲ *Traditional methods of farming are still used in the south-east (Rhône Valley) and north-east (Alsace) to harvest grapes and fruit. In the north and centre, cereal farming is highly mechanized and farms are much bigger. Many smaller, family-run farms cannot compete with them.*

in the world, with 56 million tourists in 1992. Many holiday-makers spend time in Paris, or in the ski-ing resorts in the Alps, or on the beaches in the south. But there is much more to the country than a place to spend a holiday.

This book is an introduction to France. In it you will find information about the country and its people, the climate and natural resources, how French people earn their living and spend their leisure time, and how they see the future of their country within Europe.

# FRANCE AT A GLANCE

- Area: 551,602 square kilometres
- Number of regions: 22
- Population (1993 estimate): 57.5 million
- Population density: 101.5 people per sq km
- Capital: Paris, population 9.3 million
- Other main cities: Lyon 1.2 million; Marseille 1.2 million; Lille 960,000
- Highest mountain: Mont Blanc, 4,807 metres
- Longest river: Loire, 1,012 kilometres
- Language: French
- Major religion: Christianity (77% of the French are Catholics)
- Life expectancy: 81.1 years for women (world record) and 73 years for men
- Currency: French francs, written as FF. One franc is divided into 100 centimes
- Economy: Highly industrialized. Agriculture is declining, but France has the highest production of wine in the world
- Major resources: Hydro-electricity, nuclear energy, aluminium
- Major products: Cars, aerospace products, manufactured goods, chemicals, tourism, financial services
- Environmental problems: Air and water pollution from industrial and human waste

◀ *The huge Arc de Triomphe is a landmark in Paris. In the 1950s, many people from the countryside came to Paris and other cities, looking for work and a more modern way of life.*

# THE LANDSCAPE

France is the second largest country in Europe and covers an area of 551,602 square kilometres. From north to south it measures some 973 km, and from west to east it stretches 945.5 km. It has 5,670 km of land borders, with Belgium, Germany, Switzerland, Italy, Spain, Luxembourg, Andorra and Monaco. It also has 3,120 km of coastline, of which 1,948 km are beaches.

Low and medium-sized hills and plateaux cover two-thirds of the country. Rivers cut through the hills to form deep valleys. The longest river that is entirely in France is the

▲ *The Grandes Jorasses glacier (ice field) is 4,206 metres up in Mont Blanc, near the Italian border.*

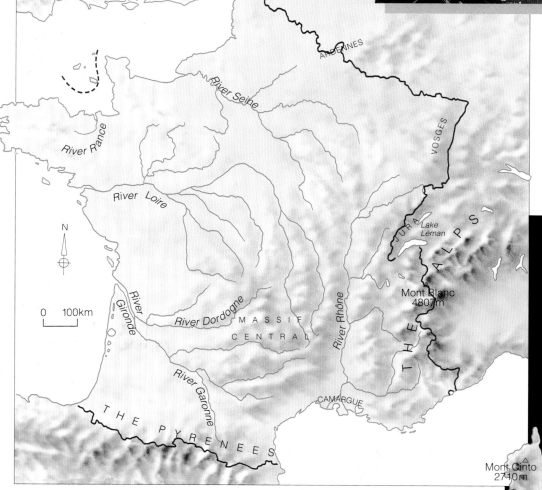

## KEY FACTS

● 25% of France is covered in forests. It is the most forested country in Europe.
● France has 150 lakes. The biggest, Lake Léman, is shared between France (234 sq km) and Switzerland (348 sq km).
● The island of Corsica covers 8,747 sq km.

*◀Languedoc Roussillon has a very varied landscape, which includes mountains, valleys and 160 km of Mediterranean beaches.*

Loire, which is 1,012 km long and flows westward across France from the Massif Central to the Atlantic Ocean. The second longest is the Seine, 776 km long, which flows north from the Bourgogne region through Paris to the English Channel. Other major rivers are the Garonne, 647 km long, flowing from the Pyrenees across the south-west of France towards the Atlantic, and the Rhône, which is 812 km long in total (500 km are in France) and flows from Switzerland down to the Mediterranean.

The mountains are very different in shape and size. The Massif Central and the Vosges are round and undulating. Their peaks, which are never higher than 1,500 metres, are often dead volcanoes. The Jura and the Alps to the east, and the Pyrenees in the south, have much higher peaks. Mont Blanc in the Alps is the highest mountain in Europe, at 4,807 metres.

The island of Corsica, 170 km off the south-east coast of mainland France, is very mountainous as well. Its highest peak, Mont Cinto, rises to 2,710 metres.

*◀The port of Saint-Malo is situated on an estuary, the point where a river flows into the sea. This estuary is 10 km long and the River Rance is 100 km long.*

# ◘ CLIMATE AND WEATHER

M ainland France lies between latitudes 42.5°N and 51°N, so it is half-way between the Equator and the North Pole. For this reason, much of the country benefits from a temperate climate, which means that it does not suffer extremes of heat or cold. Three other factors are also important: France's attachment to the continent, its closeness to the Atlantic, and its closeness to the Mediterranean.

Along the western coastline, the climate is influenced by the Atlantic. Regions to the east are more like the rest of the European continent. The southern areas have a Mediterranean climate, while the mountain regions have a different type of weather.

In the north and west, the winters are generally mild and there is very little frost. The rainfall is fairly high (70–80 cm a year) and the summers are cool. The average temperature for the year is 11–12°C. Regional variations include Normandy and Brittany in the north, where the climate is damper, with violent

▼ *At Pointe du Raz in Brittany, winds of up to 80 kph can blow along the coast for two-thirds of the time in winter and half the time in summer.*

▶ *Méribel, a ski resort in Savoie, is one of the famous "Three Valleys": the biggest ski-ing area in France, with 300 sq km of pistes.*

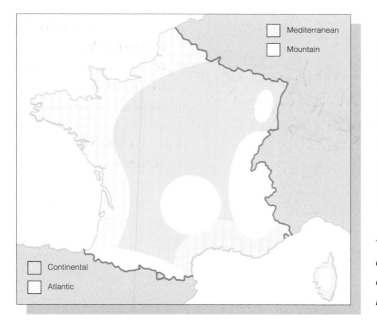

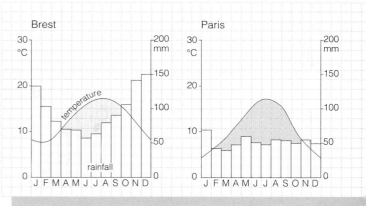

Brest

Paris

◀ **Two-thirds of France have a temperate climate, but there are 4 distinct types of climate: Atlantic, continental, Mediterranean and mountain.**

## KEY FACTS

● Without the Gulf Stream, a warm current in the Atlantic Ocean, the temperature in France would fall to -40°C in winter.
● Up to 47 metres of snow can fall at the summit of Mont Blanc in winter.
● The difference between high and low tide in Brittany can be as much as 13.5 metres, because of the shape of the seabed there.
● In the south, drought is such a problem that no rain may fall for up to 2 months.
● The wind in the south of France, called the MISTRAL, can blow at 200 kph.

winds in winter. Towards the south-west, the summers are hotter and the average temperature for the year is 13°C–14°C.

Regions in the centre of France generally have less rain. In the east, summers are hotter and winters are colder than in the west. The annual temperature in the east is 10–11°C.

The south and south-east, including Corsica, are much more like the Mediterranean countries, with very mild winters and very hot and dry summers. The average annual temperature is 14°–15°C. Most of the rain falls in autumn and spring. The French call the south of France "the midi" (meaning midday, the time when the sun is really hot).

The mountain regions have their own climate. The higher the mountains, the greater the amount of rain that falls. The average rainfall here is 1–2 metres a year, and there is heavy snow in winter.

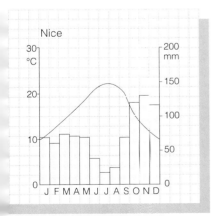

◀ In Saint-Jean Cap Ferrat, close to Nice in the south, rain may not fall for up to 320 days a year. In July and August the average land temperature is 24°C and the average temperature of the water is 26°C.

# NATURAL RESOURCES

◀ *France has constructed many dams in the Alps, on the River Rhône and in the Massif Central. The Tignes Dam in the Alps is famous for the painting on its wall, which was done with the assistance of computers.*

Each year, France consumes 2.5% of the total energy used by people on the planet. Much of its supplies are imported, although the country does have four energy sources of its own. The first is coal. Until about 1960 coal-mining was a major industry. However, because foreign coal and petrol are cheaper, there are now very few mines left in the country.

The second power source is oil and gas. Production is mainly in the south-west of France, but it is now in decline. So France has to import much of its petrol from the North Sea, the Middle East and Africa.

Hydro-electricity is the third source. Water power used to account for half of the electricity generated in France, but today its share has fallen to less than 13%.

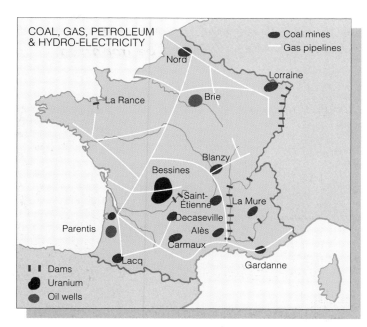

COAL, GAS, PETROLEUM & HYDRO-ELECTRICITY
● Coal mines
— Gas pipelines

Nord
Lorraine
La Rance
Brie
Blanzy
Bessines
Saint-Étienne
La Mure
Decaseville
Alès
Parentis
Carmaux
Lacq
Gardanne

Ⅱ Dams
● Uranium
● Oil wells

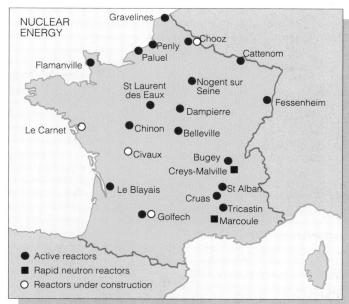

NUCLEAR ENERGY

Gravelines
Penly
Chooz
Paluel
Cattenom
Flamanville
St Laurent des Eaux
Nogent sur Seine
Fessenheim
Dampierre
Le Carnet
Chinon
Belleville
Civaux
Bugey
Creys-Malville
Le Blayais
St Alban
Cruas
Tricastin
Golfech
Marcoule

● Active reactors
■ Rapid neutron reactors
○ Reactors under construction

The fourth energy source, nuclear power, has become the main source of electricity in France. It contributes 74.5% of all the electricity that is generated there. France is very rich in uranium, which is the source of nuclear power. Nuclear power stations need only a few kilos of uranium fuel to produce electricity, instead of thousands of tonnes of oil or coal.

Experimental sources of energy which could be important in the future include solar, tidal and wind power, and energy from hot springs. There is a solar power station in the Pyrenees, and wind and tidal power stations in Brittany.

# KEY FACTS

● In 1950 France produced 65% of the energy the country required. Today it produces 47%.

● Of all the electricity generated in France, nuclear power contributes 74.5%: the highest proportion in the world.

● Despite France's extensive forests, it still has to import timber.

◀ *France is the second largest producer of nuclear electricity in the world after the USA.*

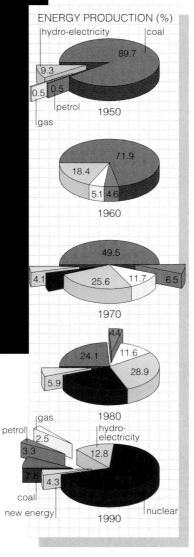

ENERGY PRODUCTION (%)

hydro-electricity | coal

89.7
9.3
0.5 0.5
petrol 1950
gas

71.9
18.4
5.1 4.6
1960

49.5
4.1 | 25.6 | 11.7 | 6.5
1970

4.4
24.1 | 11.6
5.9 | 28.9
1980

gas
petrol 2.5
3.3
hydro-electricity
12.8
7.6
coal 4.3
new energy | 1990 | nuclear

▲ *The experimental solar power station in Odeillo in the south-west of France was constructed in 1968. Its capacity is 1,000 kilowatts of electricity.*

◀ *Since the 1970s, nuclear power has become by far the most important form of energy produced in France. The country's declining supplies of coal and oil provide energy to produce metals from raw materials and to drive machines. Petrol has to be imported.*

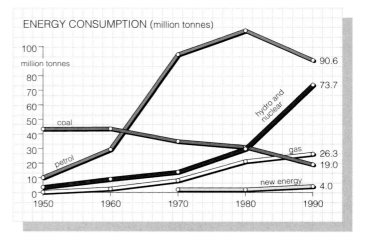

ENERGY CONSUMPTION (million tonnes)

100
million tonnes
80
70
60
50 coal
40
30 petrol
20
10
0
1950 | 1960 | 1970 | 1980 | 1990

hydro and nuclear | 90.6
73.7
gas | 26.3
19.0
new energy | 4.0

# ⊔ POPULATION

9,318,000

| | | |
|---|---|---|
| | 1,262,000 | Paris |
| | 1,231,000 | Lyon |
| | 960,000 | Marseille |
| | 696,000 | Lille |
| POPULATIONS OF | 650,000 | Bordeaux |
| THE 10 MAJOR | | Toulouse |
| CITIES AND THEIR | 517,000 | Nice |
| SUBURBS | 496,000 | Nantes |
| (1990) | 436,000 | Toulon |
| | 405,000 | Grenoble |

**F**rance used to have the highest population in Europe, and in 1850 it was the fifth most populated country in the world. Although its population has increased by 40% since the Second World War, today France is only the 20th most populated land, because of the higher growth in Third World countries.

## REGIONAL DIFFERENCES
The physical features of French people tend to vary according to regions. People in the north are generally tall with fair hair and blue eyes. In the east, most have dark eyes and hair. In the south, people tend to be smaller with dark hair and eyes.

These differences are due to the fact that the origins of the French people are very

▲ *In comparison with other European countries, there is a huge difference between the size of the capital and other cities.*

▼ *The last census, in 1990, showed that the population was approaching 57 million. This figure does not include the 2 million people living in* OVERSEAS TERRITORIES.

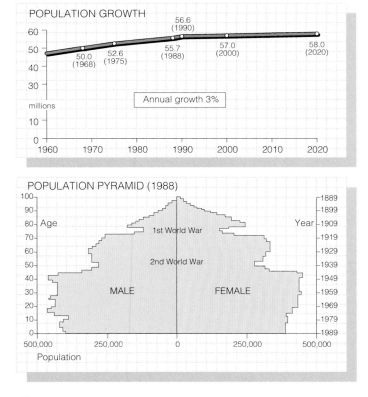

POPULATION GROWTH

- 56.6 (1990)
- 50.0 (1968)
- 52.6 (1975)
- 55.7 (1988)
- 57.0 (2000)
- 58.0 (2020)

Annual growth 3%

millions

POPULATION PYRAMID (1988)

Age — Year

1st World War

2nd World War

MALE    FEMALE

Population

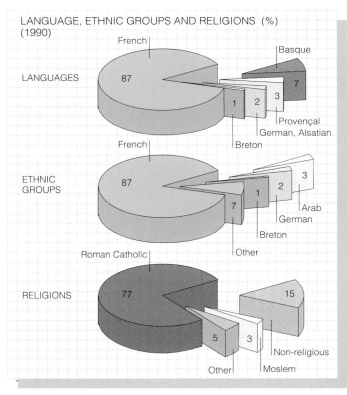

LANGUAGE, ETHNIC GROUPS AND RELIGIONS (%)
(1990)

LANGUAGES — French 87, 1, 2, 3, 7 Basque, Provençal, German, Alsatian, Breton, French

ETHNIC GROUPS — French 87, 7, 1, 2, 3 Arab, German, Breton, Other

RELIGIONS — Roman Catholic 77, 15, 5, 3 Non-religious, Moslem, Other

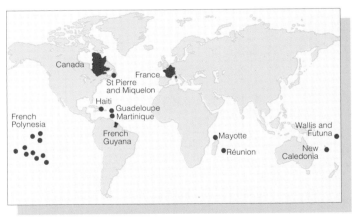

*The* OVERSEAS DEPARTMENT *of Martinique has a population of 324,000. Fort de France is the principal city. The majority of the people of Martinique are a mixture of local people and settlers who moved there from France.*

diverse. Centuries ago, Celts, Germans, Romans, Moslems and Vikings all settled in France. Later, Jewish people, Russians, and people from South-East Asia, the Middle East and North Africa also came to live there, either as refugees or to find work. Today, some languages or dialects like Breton, Basque, Catalan, Corse and Alsacian still survive as proof of people's different origins.

Each region has its own festivals or annual celebrations, including musical performances and historical parades. Many also have religious festivals at Christmas and Easter. In Alsace, for instance, there is a Christmas market at Strasbourg and an annual wine festival at Riquewihr. Very often during these festivals, people wear traditional costumes or sing and dance

*French is not only spoken in France. It is spoken in other European countries, such as Belgium, and in parts of Africa. It is also the language of the overseas departments and territories, and the official language of Quebec and New Brunswick in Canada.*

17

traditional songs.

Some regions are more populated than others. Most people tend to live where they think they will be more likely to find a job; that is, around Paris in the centre of France, or in the Rhône-Alpes region in the south-east. Others choose the south of France because of its climate.

## CITY AND COUNTRYSIDE

As in other developed European countries, this search for work means that many people leave the countryside to live in cities. In France, 73% of people live in a town or city.

But not all French people leave their villages. Recently, it has been noticed that people who have always lived in the far remote countryside tend to remain there. Others, who used to live in large cities such as Paris or Marseille, have moved to the countryside nearby. Better transport means that they can live in the country and travel to work in the city. Still others choose to live in the suburbs.

▲ **Alsace is a very traditional region of France. Children and adults wear folk costumes during festivals and celebrations.**

## KEY FACTS

● Each day in France, 2,080 babies are born.
● 3,000 French people are more than 100 years old.
● 5.7% of the population are under 3 years old; 10% are aged 8–14; 15.5% are 15–25; 48.8% are 26–59; 20% are over 60.
● 43% of French people are available for work, and 86% of these people have a job.
● 3.9% of the world's population speak French as their first language.

▼ **From 1850 onwards, people began to move to the cities. After the 1980s some areas of countryside, especially in the mountains, were deserted.**

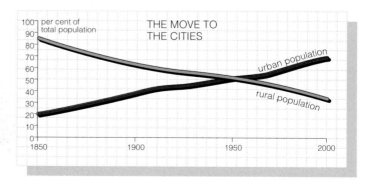

## MAIN COMPONENTS OF IMMIGRANTS (1954 AND 1982)

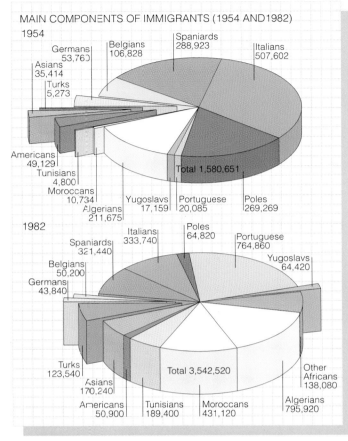

1954

Germans 53,760
Belgians 106,828
Spaniards 288,923
Italians 507,602
Asians 35,414
Turks 5,273
Americans 49,129
Tunisians 4,800
Moroccans 10,734
Algerians 211,675
Yugoslavs 17,159
Portuguese 20,085
Poles 269,269

Total 1,580,651

1982

Italians 333,740
Spaniards 321,440
Poles 64,820
Portuguese 764,860
Belgians 50,200
Germans 43,840
Yugoslavs 64,420
Turks 123,540
Asians 170,240
Americans 50,900
Tunisians 189,400
Moroccans 431,120
Algerians 795,920
Other Africans 138,080

Total 3,542,520

## 20TH CENTURY IMMIGRATION

The population of France includes about 4 million immigrants. They too live mostly in the centre, south and south-east. There is also a large immigrant population in Alsace in the east. Very often, they live in the suburbs in groups of purpose-built flats, called CITÉS, which are frequently overcrowded and run down.

Many of the immigrants come from countries in North Africa (Tunisia, Algeria, Morocco). They are known as MAGHRÉBINS.

◀ *In the 1950s, most immigrants came from Europe, especially Poland, Spain and Italy. Nowadays, many still come from Europe, but more people from North Africa are also settling in France.*

▼ *Many North African people arrive in the port of Marseille to look for work in France. Most retain their religion, Islam.*

# DAILY LIFE

The French work an average of 38 hours a week. They start relatively early in the morning, at around 6 or 7 am. At lunchtime they usually take a break of one or two hours and most of the shops are closed at that time. The working day generally finishes later than in the UK. Offices and shops tend to close between 6 and 7 pm. In the cities, people spend a lot of time sitting outside the cafés, eating, drinking and watching the world go by.

### RELIGION

Almost 80% of French people say they are Catholics, but 51% do not practise their religion. The second major religion is Islam. About 3–5 million French people are Moslems. Only 2% are Protestants.

### SPORT AND LEISURE

Several famous sporting events take place in France, including the annual Tour de France cycling competition, motor-racing at Le Mans, and the Rolland Garros tennis

▲ *France now has 70,000 cafés, down from 200,000 in 1960. Many have been replaced by fast-food restaurants. But they are still popular meeting places.*

# KEY FACTS

● 1 million books are sold in France every day.
● 67% of French teenagers have a walkman.
● 88% of French people have been to the cinema at least once in their lives.
● On average, 19% of people in Europe go away on holiday more than once a year, but in France the figure is 27% (the highest in Europe).
● Only 12% of French people take an annual holiday abroad.

## RELIGIOUS DAYS AND HOLIDAYS

| | |
|---|---|
| January 1 | JOUR DE L'AN<br>New Year's Day |
| February | MARDI GRAS<br>Carnival held on Shrove Tuesday |
| April | EASTER<br>Sunday after the first Spring full moon |
| May 1 | FÊTE DU TRAVAIL<br>Labour Day |
| 8 | ARMISTICE DAY<br>Celebration of the end of the Second World War |
| May or June | ASCENSION DAY<br>40 days after Easter |
| June | PENTECOST<br>Seventh Monday after Easter |
| July 14 | NATIONAL DAY<br>Celebration of the fall of the Bastille in 1789 |
| August 15 | ASSUMPTION<br>Celebration of the Virgin Mary |
| November 1 | TOUSSAINT (All Saint's Day) |
| 2 | FÊTE DES MORTS (All Soul's Day) |
| 11 | FÊTE DU 11 NOVEMBRE<br>Celebration of the end of the First World War |
| December 25 | NOËL (Christmas Day) |

tournament. However, the French are not really a sporty nation. Only about a fifth are members of sports clubs. Young people generally take part in a sport more often than their parents do. Jogging, aerobics, tennis, horse-riding, ski-ing, squash and golf are winning some young people away from traditional games such as BOULES or rugby. Football is now only the seventh most popular sport. It is also very fashionable in France to become involved in new sports like hang gliding, climbing or baseball. But of all sports, swimming is the one that most French people are likely to practise.

About 95% of French people have a TV set, and on average they watch three and a quarter hours a day. Although they do not go to the cinema as often as they used to, nevertheless the French have the fourth highest figure in the world for cinema attendance, after China, the USA and

▲ *The game of boules became popular in the south of France in the 19th century. Older people tend to play more, but many young people also take part in competitions.*

▶ *There are 1,773 rugby clubs in France. The cockerel, which symbolizes the fighting spirit in France, is the emblem of the national rugby team. Many fans come to matches carrying flags and a cockerel. The rugby stadium in Paris, the Parc des Princes, is one of the most famous.*

India. Sophisticated new cinemas are being built — for example, the Geode in Paris, which has a 1,000 square metre hemispherical screen.

## EDUCATION

School is compulsory between the ages of 6 and 16. Some children start earlier, going to nursery school, which is called "la maternelle", when they are 2 years old. Between the ages of 6 and 11 they go to primary school. Then they attend the local secondary school, known as "le collège".

At the age of 15, pupils sit their first national examination, "le Brevet des collèges". They can then decide whether they want to continue their academic education or learn a skill to get a job. Those who leave can go to a "lycée technique" for training and may work part-time as apprentices while they train. Those who stay at school study at the "lycée", where at the age of 18 they take the BACCALAURÉAT,

▲ *The Eiffel Tower, 320 metres high, was built in 1889. It is a famous landmark in Paris. Visitors often go up the tower in a lift, or travel past it in a* BATEAU MOUCHE *along the Seine.*

◄ *The Cannes film festival takes place each year in May. Actors and directors from all over the world present their films and a jury of experts judges which is the best. While the festival is taking place, fans queue for hours to catch a glimpse of their favourite stars.*

# KEY FACTS

● 41% of French people speak no other languages except French.

● More than 3 million French adults cannot read or write.

● In France, primary schoolchildren spend an average of 27 hours a week at school; secondary school pupils spend 30.5 hours a week there (in the UK, the figures are 21 and 22 hours).

● Most primary schoolchildren and some secondary schoolchildren go to school on Saturday mornings.

the equivalent of 'A' levels in the UK. If they pass this, they can go to university.

Since 1972 schoolchildren have not attended school on Wednesday afternoons. Instead they do sporting activities or attend youth clubs. Otherwise they only have 2 or 3 hours of sport a week at school.

Young people in France are better off in terms of school holidays in comparison with their European neighbours. The academic year starts in September, after a nine-week summer holiday. Schoolchildren also have the usual breaks at other times of the year. To compensate for all this free time, pupils usually start school at 8 am and have an hour's lunch break between 1 and 2 pm, finishing at 5 pm.

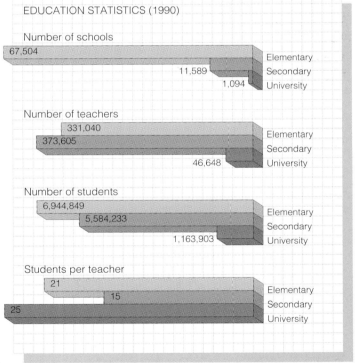

EDUCATION STATISTICS (1990)

| Number of schools | |
|---|---|
| 67,504 | Elementary |
| 11,589 | Secondary |
| 1,094 | University |

| Number of teachers | |
|---|---|
| 331,040 | Elementary |
| 373,605 | Secondary |
| 46,648 | University |

| Number of students | |
|---|---|
| 6,944,849 | Elementary |
| 5,584,233 | Secondary |
| 1,163,903 | University |

| Students per teacher | |
|---|---|
| 21 | Elementary |
| 15 | Secondary |
| 25 | University |

◀ *Schooling is free up until the equivalent of GCSE level. If pupils stay on until they are 18, they have to buy their own school books.*

# RULE AND LAW

*◀The Palace of Versailles was the home of French monarchs and the centre of political life in the 17th and 18th centuries.*

*▼The National Assembly and the Senate vote to decide the laws. If there is a disagreement, the National Assembly has the last word.*

In 1789 the French Revolution overthrew the monarchy in France and created the National Assembly. The First Republic of France was proclaimed in 1792. The Fifth Republic was set up in 1958.

The head of state is the President of the Republic, who is elected for seven years. The President's powers include appointing a Prime Minister, who is the chief of government and puts the policies of the President into practice. If the President and Prime Minister belong to opposing parties, this can cause conflicts.

Parliament is composed of the National Assembly and the Senate. The National Assembly deputies are directly elected by all French people over the age of 18, and they serve five-year terms. Adults in the overseas departments also vote in these elections. Members of the Senate are elected for nine-year terms by regional representatives and the National Assembly, or sometimes the National Assembly votes to transfer one of its deputies to the Senate.

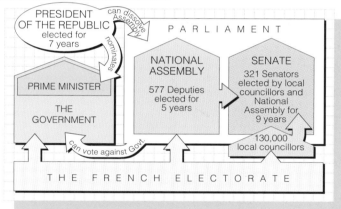

PRESIDENT OF THE REPUBLIC
elected for 7 years
can dissolve Assembly
nominates

PARLIAMENT

PRIME MINISTER
THE GOVERNMENT

NATIONAL ASSEMBLY
577 Deputies elected for 5 years

SENATE
321 Senators elected by local councillors and National Assembly for 9 years

can vote against Govt.

130,000 local councillors

THE FRENCH ELECTORATE

The chief political parties are the Socialist Party (PS), Communist Party (PC), Republican Party (RPR) and Democratic Union (UDF). Others include two green parties, Les Verts and Génération Écologie. In the regional elections of 1992, their combined share of the vote was the highest (14.4%) it had ever been.

Since 1972, France has been divided into 22 regions, each of which includes between two and seven departments. Regional elections were introduced in 1981. These elections have given more power to the regions and the mayors of the towns to make local decisions.

◀ *Each village and town of France has a mayor, whose job includes taking decisions about the economy of the town, liaising with the police and conducting wedding ceremonies.*

## KEY FACTS

● At the age of 18, all French men are eligible for national service (basic military training).

● The death penalty was abolished in 1981.

● In 1992 Edith Cresson became the first woman Prime Minister of France. There has never yet been a woman President.

● In 1989 the murder rate in France was 4.1 per 100,000 people, compared with 1.3 in the UK and 8.6 in the USA.

▶ *There are two police forces in France. One is the gendarmerie, a military force, whose duties include guarding public buildings.*

▶ *The other national police force includes a unit called the CRS. Its 5,000 officers are used to break up riots and demonstrations. They use tear gas, helmets and riot shields.*

# FOOD AND FARMING

*The French tend to spend a lot of time over their main meal, which is eaten in the evening. It has at least 4 courses — a starter, a meat or fish dish with vegetables, cheese and a dessert.*

## KEY FACTS

● France grows 57 million tonnes of cereals (including rice) – a third of all cereal production in the European Community.
● It produces 10% of the world's sugar beet.
● In 1990 France imported 122,000 tonnes of tobacco.
● 60% of French people drink tea without any milk.
● 50% of French people keep wine in their cellars.

Before the First World War, one out of every two French people was a farmer; today the figure is only one out of 12 and many of these are only part-time farmers. However, France has the highest agricultural production of any country in Europe and a quarter of all the farmed land in the European Community.

Since the end of the Second World War, farming has become much more mechanized. Today France is the fourth largest manufacturer of tractors in the world (1.4 million a year) and it builds other large agricultural machines too. These need to be operated in large fields if they are to be efficient. So the 40% of French farms which cover less than 10 hectares are gradually giving way to farms which cover more than 50 hectares. The very big farms covering more than 200 hectares already represent 7% of the country's farmland.

Different areas have different sorts of farms. In the colder, wetter mountain regions, cattle, sheep and goats graze on

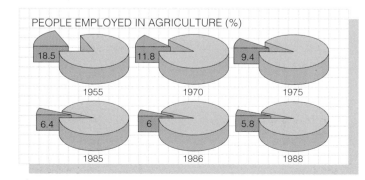

PEOPLE EMPLOYED IN AGRICULTURE (%)

| 18.5 | 11.8 | 9.4 |
|------|------|-----|
| 1955 | 1970 | 1975 |
| 6.4  | 6    | 5.8 |
| 1985 | 1986 | 1988 |

the grass in summer. In the north and centre, the cool, damp conditions are ideal for growing plants for animal fodder, sugar beet, cereals and crops such as sunflowers, whose seeds are used to make cooking oil. In 1990 the country produced 2.3 million tonnes of sunflower seed.

France is Europe's most important producer of cereals and it ranks sixth in the world in this. The main cereals are wheat, barley and maize. Wheat is grown in the north of the country. It is used to make bread, pastries and pastas and is also exported to other European countries. In 1990, wheat production was 33.5 million tonnes. Maize and barley are grown in the centre of France and are chiefly used to feed cattle.

In 1990 France produced more wine than any other country in the world – 66.5 million

► **Although France imports citrus fruits, orange and lemon trees do grow in the south. An annual festival of oranges and lemons is held in Menton.**

◄ **Alsace in the east produces a lot of white wine. The centre, west and south-east primarily produce red wine.**

► **In the past 20 years, France has produced 50–75 million hectolitres of wine a year. It is a major export.**

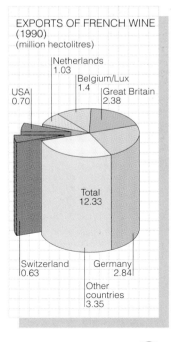

EXPORTS OF FRENCH WINE (1990)
(million hectolitres)

Netherlands 1.03
Belgium/Lux 1.4
USA 0.70
Great Britain 2.38
Total 12.33
Switzerland 0.63
Germany 2.84
Other countries 3.35

hectolitres. Grapes are an important crop in most regions. The competition is fierce, but the very high quality of French wines ensures that they find an export market.

Fruit and vegetables are mostly grown in the sunnier, Mediterranean-type climate of the south, especially in Provence, as well as in the western and northern areas such as Brittany and the Loire Valley. France is the third largest producer of these foods in Europe, but Spain and Italy are far ahead. The most important fruits are apples, peaches, plums, apricots, cherries and strawberries. Recently, farmers in the south have also begun to grow kiwi fruits.

Vegetables include tomatoes, cauliflowers, carrots, lettuces, onions and beans. But France still imports a large quantity of tropical and citrus fruit.

French people eat a good deal of meat. Generally they eat more pork and chicken than beef, which explains why the number of beef cattle has declined while pig raising and poultry production have increased. However, although some beef cattle are kept in most regions of France, pig rearing is concentrated in the west, especially in Brittany. It is a highly industrialized activity.

All countries which are members of the European Community share a common

▶ *Tuna, whiting, sardines, hake and cod form the main part of the French fishing catch. Shellfish such as lobsters and crabs are also popular. In restaurants, seafood dishes are very elaborate and appetizing.*

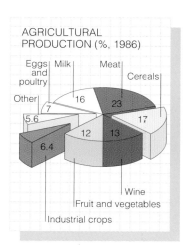

AGRICULTURAL PRODUCTION (%, 1986)

Eggs and poultry

Milk

Meat

Cereals

Other

7

16

23

17

5.6

12

13

6.4

Wine

Fruit and vegetables

Industrial crops

▲*A window display in a French* PÂTISSERIE. *French cakes include cream puffs, which are traditionally eaten at weddings and christenings.*

▲*About 80% of French people eat bread every day.* BAGUETTES *(French stick) are the most traditional bread.*

policy on agriculture. Some regulations are very strict, as they are intended to make sure that prices are much the same across the member states and that there is a balance between imports and exports. The French government sometimes has to limit the production of some products, which causes conflicts between farmers

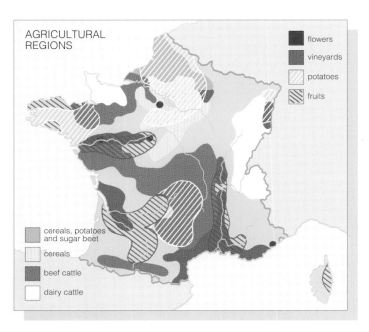

AGRICULTURAL
REGIONS

- flowers
- vineyards
- potatoes
- fruits

- cereals, potatoes and sugar beet
- cereals
- beef cattle
- dairy cattle

and the state.

Nowadays French people do not spend as much time eating breakfast or lunch, and many young people eat cereals, use ketchup and eat less bread and croissants than previous generations did. Although wine consumption has fallen, the French still drink more wine than any other people in the world, except for the Portuguese and Italians.

Each region of France has its own food speciality. For example, in Alsace in the east, "choucroute" is a famous dish of cabbage in white wine with pork and sausages. In the west people eat a lot of seafood. In central France, "boeuf bourguignon" is a very famous dish of beef in a red wine sauce. The Rhône Valley has delicacies which include "saucissons" (dried sausage). The south has a Mediterranean-type of cuisine, with a lot of garlic and vegetables such as courgettes, aubergines, tomatoes and herbs. These are used to make the vegetable stew called "ratatouille".

# TRADE AND INDUSTRY

France is a highly industrialized country. But some traditional industries, such as metallurgy, textiles and ship-building, are now in decline, although the car, chemical and electrical industries are still very strong. New businesses include aeronautics and pharmaceuticals.

## SMELTING AND MANUFACTURING

Smelting, the production of metals from ores, was an important industry in France for a long time. Nowadays most of the mines are closed, although France is still Europe's leading producer of bauxite, the ore from which aluminium is made. However, smelting does still exist, relying mostly on imported raw materials. The French smelter Usinor-Sacilor is the second largest in the world.

France's manufacturing industry is vast. It produces heavy goods such as engines, ovens, turbines for nuclear power stations, machines for agriculture and the building industry, and lighter goods which include medical and optical equipment. Despite the size of this industry, its production is small compared to that of the leading countries, which contribute 70% of world production.

◀ *La Défense in Paris is the centre for business, trade and industry. Here, 100,000 people work every day in the area's numerous skyscrapers.*

▶ *The French state aerospace company, Aérospatiale, plans to launch the Ariane V rocket in 1995 from the launching site in French Guyana.*

## SUCCESSFUL INDUSTRIES

'High-tech' industries such as aeronautics and space technology are leading enterprises in France. France's aerospace industry is the third largest in the world. It is involved with the Hermes project, which aims to launch a space-shuttle carrying three astronauts into space early in the 21st century.

The state invests in many research projects and some are run in partnership with other European countries. The supersonic airliner Concorde was a joint venture between France and the United Kingdom; the last Airbus airliner was developed by France, Germany, Spain and the UK. France has also been involved in building helicopters, missiles and, above all, the Ariane rocket. France is currently developing a highly advanced

# KEY FACTS

● France's car industry employs about 10% of the working population.
● Only 24 factories in France each employ more than 5,000 people.
● The pharmaceutical industry is expanding. In the last 15 years, 100 new products have been launched.
● French people spend an average of £170 each on medicines a year.

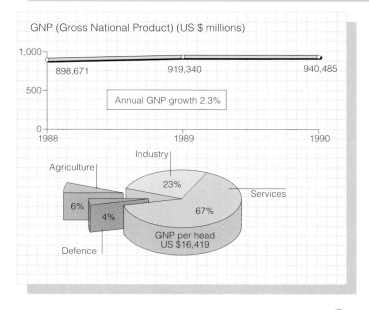

GNP (Gross National Product) (US $ millions)

| | 898,671 | 919,340 | 940,485 |

Annual GNP growth 2.3%

1988     1989     1990

Agriculture 6%
Defence 4%
Industry 23%
Services 67%
GNP per head US $16,419

▶ *France's manufacturing industry is very varied, ranging from cars to paper products.*

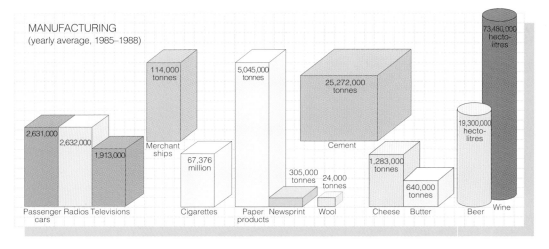

MANUFACTURING
(yearly average, 1985–1988)

- Passenger cars: 2,631,000
- Radios: 2,632,000
- Televisions: 1,913,000
- Merchant ships: 114,000 tonnes
- Cigarettes: 67,376 million
- Paper products: 5,045,000 tonnes
- Newsprint: 305,000 tonnes
- Wool: 24,000 tonnes
- Cement: 25,272,000 tonnes
- Cheese: 1,283,000 tonnes
- Butter: 640,000 tonnes
- Beer: 19,300,000 hecto-litres
- Wine: 73,480,000 hecto-litres

military aircraft.

The car industry is the fourth largest in the world after those in Japan, the United States and Germany. Most French cars are sold in Europe, especially in Italy and Spain.

The chemical industry includes a large variety of goods – from paint and plastics, to medicine and beauty products. The pharmaceuticals industry is developing rapidly. As for beauty products, for many years France has been the leading producer of luxury perfumes. Several of these are made by leading clothing firms.

Make-up, hair products and toiletries are also important.

## TEXTILES AND TOURISM

Clothing designers such as Coco Chanel, Yves Saint-Laurent, Cacharel and Christian Dior are famous all around the world. The textile industry is one of the oldest in France, but it has had its problems. In 1980, France had to import more textile products than it exported for the first time in its history. Although its textile industry is the second largest in Europe, after Italy, it is in recession.

*Many industries use electricity generated by nuclear power. Some 13% of France's electricity production is exported.*

## KEY FACTS

● Bauxite originates from Baux in Provence, the place where it was first extracted.
● France produces a very small amount of gold: just one four-hundredth of world production.
● Ship-building has collapsed in France due to competition from Japan, Korea and other Far Eastern countries.
● France is the third largest exporter of cars in the world after Japan and Germany. The most popular car sold in France recently has been the Peugeot 205.

This is partly because of competition from very cheap products from Third World countries. Only luxury textile products are still produced very profitably in France.

With its historic monuments, cultural centres and natural beauty, France attracts many tourists. "Blue tourism" means holidays at the seaside and is the most important type of tourism in France. "Green tourism" refers to holidays in the countryside and the mountains. This form of tourism attracts more and more people who are either looking for tranquillity or for a sporting holiday. In 1992, France had almost as many foreign tourists as it has inhabitants — about 56 million. The hotel industry, which 30 years ago was very old fashioned, is now the third largest in Europe.

*Several of France's clothing designers are very famous. Here, Yves Saint-Laurent poses at a fashion show with a model, Lucie de la Falaise.*

*The perfume industry is based in Paris and in the south of France.*

► *The Airbus
airliners were
developed by
Aérospatiale of
France, British
Aerospace (UK),
MBB (Germany)
and Casa (Spain).
By the middle of
1991, a total of
723 Airbuses
were operating
throughout the
world. Today
1,770 people are
employed on the
project in France,
including 1,284
in Toulouse.*

◄ *Ship-building
in France is an
industry in
decline. In the
mid-1980s it
employed 22,000
people, but today
the figure is only
6,600.*

# TRANSPORT

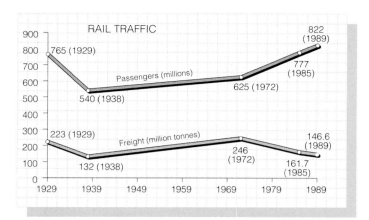

### RAIL TRAFFIC

Passengers (millions)
765 (1929)
540 (1938)
625 (1972)
777 (1985)
822 (1989)

Freight (million tonnes)
223 (1929)
132 (1938)
246 (1972)
161.7 (1985)
146.6 (1989)

1929  1939  1949  1959  1969  1979  1989

### RAIL NETWORK

Calais
Lille
Paris
Le Mans
Tours
Lyon

electric trains
||||TGVs

The French government sees transport as a priority. The railway system, the road system and air transport have all been improved and are now among the best in the European Community.

In 1981, the launch of the high-speed train, the TGV ("train à grande vitesse"), was a huge success. The train operates at 300 kph and covers the 500 km between Paris and Lyon in less than two hours. It is so effective that some people now work in Paris and live in Lyon. This success encouraged the French railway company, the Société Nationale des Chemins de Fer

▼ *The TGV, developed in 1981, has broken the world rail speed record with a top speed of 515 kph.*

(SNCF), to build many new lines as quickly as possible. Today, the TGV runs from Paris to other cities such as Rennes in the north-west, Le Mans in the centre of France and Bordeaux in the south-west. But the project doesn't end in France. The high-speed train travels between Paris and London in just three hours. It also reaches cities in Italy and Belgium.

The SNCF is the most important transport enterprise in France. The cost of developing a project such as the TGV is enormous, but the state has provided much of the money. Across France as a whole, the number of people travelling by train is slowly increasing, although the volume of goods transported is decreasing.

Despite their fine railway system, the

## KEY FACTS

● To run the TGV, France has had to build 185 new bridges, 315 new railway bridges, 9 viaducts, 2 bridges across main rivers and 2 new stations.

● Air France is the biggest airline in France. It flies between 80 different countries.

● In 1990 road accidents in France left 10,300 people dead and 226,000 injured – double the figures for the UK.

● In the year 2000 there will be 11,300 km of motorways in France, compared with 7,110 km in 1989.

● With the Channel Tunnel completed, a railway shuttle carrying 200 cars and 35 lorries will leave Paris or London every 3 minutes during peak times, so more than 4,000 vehicles an hour will be carried through the tunnel in each direction.

◀ *France and Britain began work on the Channel Tunnel in 1985. It is 50.5 km long and opened in 1994. The plan is for railway shuttles, each 800 metres long, to carry cars and foot passengers through the tunnel. Using TGVs could cut the journey time between Paris and London to 3 hours and 15 minutes.*

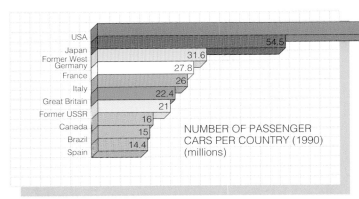

| | | NUMBER OF PASSENGER CARS PER COUNTRY (1990) (millions) |
|---|---|---|
| USA | 54.5 | 186 |
| Japan | 31.6 | |
| Former West Germany | 27.8 | |
| France | 26 | |
| Italy | 22.4 | |
| Great Britain | 21 | |
| Former USSR | 16 | |
| Canada | 15 | |
| Brazil | 14.4 | |
| Spain | | |

▼ *A quarter of all new cars bought in France in 1991 were made by Renault. One of its latest cars, the Renault Clio, is a small car designed to be used in the city. Renault is the second largest French car manufacturer, after Peugeot Citroën.*

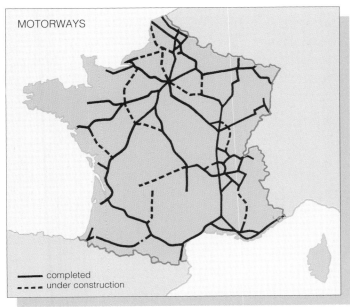

MOTORWAYS

—— completed
- - - - under construction

Despite their fine railway system, the French still prefer to travel by car. There are 27.8 million cars on the road in France. If all these vehicles were placed end to end, the line would stretch four times around the world. Only the United States, Japan and Germany have more vehicles than France. The motorways are not free in France: all motorists have to pay at a toll station to use them, so travelling by motorway is quite expensive. But the road system is very efficient.

Air travel is increasingly popular in France. Over the last 30 years, Charles de Gaulle Airport outside Paris has become the eighth busiest airport in the world, in terms of the number of passengers it handles.

Many goods which arrive in or leave France are sent by sea. The port of Le Havre-Rouen handles the transport of goods through the English Channel, Dunkerque handles those that go by the North Sea, and Marseille those that go through the Mediterranean. Transport by river is still very important for some products such as cement, coal and cereals. France has 8,568 km of navigable waterways. But few people travel by sea, unless they are only going short distances, for example across to Corsica or to Britain.

# THE ENVIRONMENT

In order to become a leading industrial power, France built factories, dams and nuclear power stations without giving too much thought to their effect on the environment. Land has been cleared, plant and animal species have been destroyed and pollution has increased. Recently, the French have become more concerned about these problems.

One of the major environmental problems is finding space for industrial waste and household rubbish. The municipal dumps are full up and towns have to take action to recycle articles such as glass and paper, or to find more space for dumps. Since 1989, many special containers for recycling glass or paper have been installed in 20,000 towns and villages. But such efforts are still very small.

Industrial waste causes the most concern. Each year France produces an average of 150 million tonnes of industrial waste. Of this figure, 18 million tonnes are poisonous waste. Most of this is disposed of in 12 special sites in France and a small amount goes to dumps in Germany. By the year 2000 these 12 sites will be full, so France will have to find new places to bury its poisonous waste.

A second environmental problem is caused by fire. Fires can break out for several different reasons. Sometimes they are caused by natural events, such as lightning; sometimes they begin because of electrical faults or because of the thoughtlessness of people who throw away lighted cigarette ends or leave their camp fires unattended. Thousands of hectares of forest are destroyed by fire each year, especially in the south.

A third problem concerns the water. Many rivers in industrial areas are so badly polluted by factories that they can no longer be used to supply drinking water. Despite stricter laws, pollution from factories continues. For example, waste from 15 factories pollutes the River Rhône, killing tonnes of fish. Recent governments have introduced measures to clean up polluted rivers. The River Seine should be cleaned up by 1994.

◄ *Members of the environmental group Greenpeace try to block discharges of waste into the River Seine from a chemical company, Rhône-Poulenc.*

▲ *Forest fires in the south of France are difficult to control when there is wind. Special flying boats take off from the coast, filling their tanks with 5,500 litres of water to dump on the fires.*

The condition of sea water is a little better. Since 1989, most French beaches have been cleaned up. But one of the most disastrous forms of pollution is caused by large oil tankers. In 1978, 220,000 tonnes of oil from the tanker *Amoco Cadiz* were spilt into the sea off Brittany. As a result, 360 km of coastline were badly damaged, 35 species of birds were affected, and 30% of oysters in the area died.

Air pollution is the fourth environmental problem, as air is badly affected by the fumes from factories and cars. More and

## KEY FACTS

● Domestic waste is a significant problem in France. For example, each year the average French person buys approximately 63 kilos of bread and throws away 9.5 kilos of it.

● A third of all glass bottles in France are recycled.

● 45% of atmospheric pollution in France is caused by factories, 29% by non-nuclear electric power stations, 15% by heating systems in towns, and 11% by transport (cars, lorries, aeroplanes, etc).

more towns are banning cars from their centres, and more people are buying cars which use lead-free petrol. Today, 59 per cent of French people say that they are prepared to use lead-free petrol even if it is more expensive. However, it is still common to see clouds of pollution above the largest French cities.

In the face of these problems, pressure for environmental protection is growing. When there is a plan to build a new ski resort, dam, railway line or factory, people who oppose the idea get together and put pressure on the government and the building companies concerned. Sometimes they succeed in having the plans changed.

French people are also concerned about the growing number of nuclear power stations in their country, especially since the accident at the power station of Chernobyl in Russia in 1986. Old power stations which have been closed down can be a danger to the community too, as radiation may remain a problem for centuries.

Because many animal species are in danger of disappearing completely from the land, the government has opened wildlife parks to protect them. France now has seven national parks and about 30 national reserves. In these parks, agricultural activities, fishing and hunting are generally banned, building is very restricted and camping and tourism are tightly controlled. During the last 30 years, 20 different animal species have been reintroduced to the country. Wolves, wild horses, bears and eagles are among those which have special protection.

◀ *In Tahiti, in French Polynesia, many campaigns are organized against the destruction of the forests and natural habitats. Marine life is also protected there.*

▶ *The Camargue, one of France's regional parks, covers 85,000 hectares in the south. Its protected species include wild horses and flamingoes.*

# THE FUTURE

For centuries, Paris was the centre of all economic and cultural activities in France. However, the government is now developing the role of the regions. It has plans to improve road and rail links all over the country, and it is also making efforts to introduce tourism to the most remote areas. Places in the countryside which have suffered as people have moved to the cities are seeing their regions revived by tourism.

The idea of building the Euro Disney Resort near Paris, which opened in 1992, shows how much France wants to attract tourists from all over the world. Other tourist sites and theme parks are opening elsewhere.

Further changes have come with the introduction of high technology. France's

© The Walt Disney Company

▶ *The Euro Disney® Resort covers 1,943 hectares (a fifth of the size of Paris), of which 600 hectares have been developed. It includes a theme park, hotels, restaurants and other attractions.*

◀ *The Futuroscope at Poitiers in the west of France is a theme park dedicated to the world of cinema. The buildings are very futuristic and they include 10 different cinemas.*

telephone system, for example, is very sophisticated. Many households now have a computer linked to their telephone. This enables them to book tickets for concerts, order their shopping, control their bank accounts, check the weather forecast, or consult job advertisements. Technological progress also means that people are more mobile and have more opportunities to travel abroad and participate in sporting activities. The French today generally have much more leisure time than previous generations did.

However, not everyone is able to benefit from these opportunities. France has to find ways to solve major problems such as unemployment, poor housing and pollution. It also has to provide care for its increasing numbers of old people and support for immigrants. Other European countries also

face these problems, and the decisions that France makes will have consequences not only for its own future but for the future of Europe as a whole.

In 1789, the French government issued a Declaration of Human and Civil Rights. Today, the top of the Arche de la Défense, the highest building in Paris, is where the International Foundation for Human Rights has its headquarters. Just as the Foundation works on global issues, so France today is not only looking inwards at its own development, it is also looking outwards to play a part in Europe and the international community.

▼ *France is part of the European Space Agency, which is developing rockets to send satellites into orbit and, eventually, to send people into space.*

## KEY FACTS

● By 2010, 13% of the French population will be more than 75 years old.
● By 2020, France will have the 24th highest population in the world.
● The French government hopes that by the year 2000, 80% of people aged 18 will take the Baccalauréat, compared with 56% now.
● Because of the growing numbers of older people, the government has invested 7 billion francs in a project to try to ensure they will have retirement benefits over the next 30 years.

# FURTHER INFORMATION

● FRENCH INSTITUTE
17 Queensberry Place, London SW7 2DT
French cultural centre, with an art gallery, theatre, cinema, library for adults and children, and video library.
● FRENCH TOURISM OFFICE
178 Piccadilly, London W1W 0AL
Provides a range of tourist information on France, including the overseas territories.
● MAISON DE LA FRANCE
8 Avenue de l'Opéra, 75 001 Paris
Provides general information on France, including dates and venues of festivals and events.

● OFFICE DE TOURISME DE PARIS
127 Champs Elysees, 75 0008 Paris
Provides tourist information on Paris, including a calendar of special events.

## BOOKS ABOUT FRANCE

*Passport to France*, Dominique Norbrook, Franklin Watts 1991 (age 8–11)
*Countries of the World: France*, Alan Blackwood and Brigitte Chosson, Wayland 1991 (age 8–11)
*Destination France*, Headway Hodder & Stoughton 1990 (age 14+)

# GLOSSARY

**BACCALAURÉAT**
An examination taken by pupils at the age of 18; equivalent to 'A' levels in the UK.

**BAGUETTE**
A long, thin stick of crusty bread, which is the most common form of bread in France.

**BÂTEAU MOUCHE**
A river boat used for sight-seeing trips.

**BOULES**
A game similar to bowls, but played with smaller, steel balls.

**CITÉ**
A large development of blocks of flats.

**MAGHRÉBINS**
Arab people from the countries of North Africa which used to be controlled by France.

**MISTRAL**
A strong wind which often blows southwards in the southern part of the Rhône Valley.

**OVERSEAS DEPARTMENTS**
Areas which are part of the French state but not part of mainland France. Their inhabitants have the same voting rights as those who live in France.

**OVERSEAS TERRITORIES**
Areas which used to be governed by France and still have strong links with it.

**PÂTISSERIE**
A French cake shop. The word is also used to mean cakes, tarts and pastries.

# INDEX

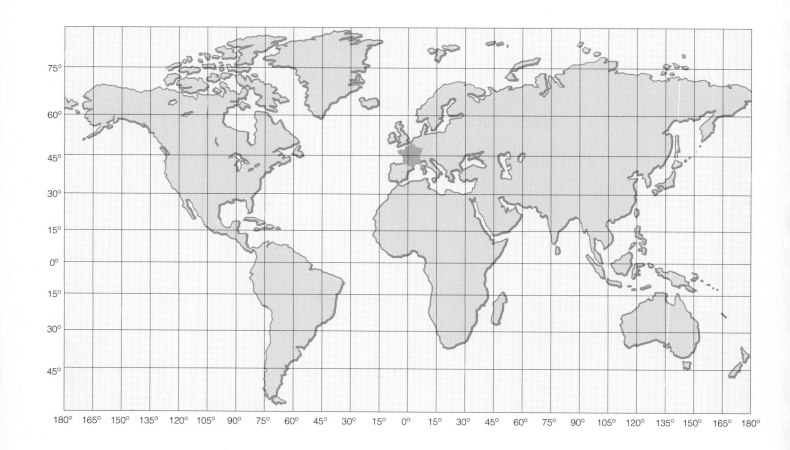

**OVERSEAS DEPARTMENTS**
GUADELOUPE in the Caribbean Sea
MARTINIQUE in the Caribbean
FRENCH GUYANA in South America
RÉUNION in the Indian Ocean
ST PIERRE AND MIQUELON in the Gulf
    of St Lawrence, Canada

**OVERSEAS TERRITORIES**
NEW CALEDONIA in the Pacific Ocean
FRENCH POLYNESIA in the Pacific
WALLIS AND FUTUNA in the Pacific
MAYOTTE in the Indian Ocean
FRENCH ANTARCTICA